THE 30-DAY TRANSFORMATION CHALLENGE

A Woman's Beginners Guide to Becoming Productive, Self-Confident, Disciplined, and Achieving Success Now

Lauren Brentley

Your Free Gift

As a way of saying thanks for your purchase, I'm offering my BOOK

Find You're Why The Key To Staying Motivated And Achieving Your Goals For FREE

To Get Instant Access,
Just Go To https://laurenbrentlybooks.com

Inside This Book, You Will Discover

- How this one strategy will help you in identifying you're why
- The one small trick to maintaining a positive attitude and self-talk
- Why this one strategy will keep you committed every single day
- And so much more

Self-Contract

On this day, _ _ _ _ _ _ _ _ _ _, I _ _ _ _ _ _ _ _ _ _ _
_ hereby commit
to giving my best effort every day as I strive to
become a more productive, self-confident and
disciplined woman.

I promise to prioritize my well-being, ensuring
that my spiritual, emotional/mental, and
physical needs are met before anyone else's.

I pledge to remain consistent on my transformation journey, even when challenges come
because I know that success will not happen if
I choose to give up.

I desire success. Therefore, I vow to complete
all the challenges within this 30-day challenge
diligently.

I will learn from every mistake and retrace my
steps where necessary. But one thing I will
never do is to give up on myself.

_ _ _ _ _ _ _ _ _ _ _ _ _ _ _ _ _ _ _

Signature

Contents

Introduction 7

How to Use This Book 10

Chapter 1: Tool Number 1: Take Charge of Your Mornings 11

Chapter 2: Tool Number 2: Relieve Stress and Negative Energy 16

Chapter 3: Tool Number 3: Affirm Yourself Daily 22

Chapter 4: Tool Number 4: Nourish Your Body 28

Chapter 5: Tool Number 5: Self-Love = Self-Care 34

Chapter 6: Tool Number 6: Forgive 41

Chapter 7: Tool Number 7: Own Your Goals 50

Chapter 8: Tool Number 8: Rest 58

Chapter 9: Tool Number 9: Mindset and Motivation... 64

Chapter 10: Tool Number 10: Exercise and Endorphins 71

Chapter 11: Tool Number 11: Discipline, Distractions, and Doing Hard Things First.. 79

Afterword... 87

About the Author................................... 91

Introduction

Have you ever seen a truly successful woman and thought, "How on planet Earth does she do that?!" Do you sometimes get lost in your thoughts, wondering what it takes to overcome a mediocre lifestyle and transform into an extraordinary woman who is highly self-confident, super productive, disciplined to the bone, and an overall success?

I also used to sit back and wonder until I got fed up with the usual and decided it was time to challenge myself toward the greatness that was calling me. The truth is, some things seem like rocket science until you actually push yourself and take things one day at a time. There are some specific tools that can help you make the necessary changes to your life. These tools are a combination of scientifically tested and proven methods, spiritually recognized concepts (no worries if you're not into all that *woo-woo* stuff), and a whole lot in between.

I have compiled these tools into my **TRANS-FORMED** Framework. Everything you'll learn within this framework is what has turned me into *that successful woman* I always envied. And I bet that is what you desire for yourself. You are tired of making excuses, constantly procrastinating, self-sabotaging, putting others before yourself, and so many other unhealthy vices. You have had enough and just want to live a life worthy of envy—one that has only happened in your dreams.

Well, I am happy to tell you that you have gotten the right book! In this short and simplified manual, I will show you how to completely transform into the woman of your dreams using my TRANSFORMED Framework. There are eleven major transformation tools, and each chapter focuses on one tool.

How to Use This Book

My TRANSFORMED Framework outlines eleven life-changing tools that necessitate your transformation. With each chapter, you'll get daily challenges to help you implement all you've learned. These challenges are not for reading only. They are to push you to actually take action. Why? Because let's face it, transformation will never happen until you get up and do the work!

The challenges total thirty (30), making this a **30-day "TRANSFORMED" Challenge**. Some days have more challenges than others. Just take it one day at a time without skipping any. So, are you ready for the transformation of your life? I believe in you! Let's begin with tool number one.

Chapter 1:
Tool Number 1: Take Charge of Your Mornings

Mornings can spell chaos for a lot of women. Whether you're a student who needs to make it to class on time, an employee who has to get ready for work, or a mom who has to go through a morning routine with grumpy kids, it can get very rushed and hectic. How you start your day can significantly impact your mood and productivity throughout the rest of the day. So, there's no better place to begin your transformation than your morning routines.

To be frank, your *ideal* morning routine will

not happen every single day — nothing in life is perfect. Your goal should be to ensure that, on most days, you are taking charge and not being swallowed by the morning rush.

How can you achieve this? Here are six-morning routine hacks that can help you feel less overwhelmed and, more importantly, get you ready to take on the day like the warrior that you are:

1. **Plan your mornings from the night before**: Lighten your morning load by taking care of some tasks the night before. For example, pick your outfit for the next day, prep breakfast, tidy up the kitchen, and write out your to-do list.

2. **Leave your phone on Do-Not-Disturb**: Waking up to notifications can quickly take you into "task mode." The first thirty minutes of your day should fuel your spirit, soul, and body, not scrolling

through work emails, terrifying news, or social media.

3. **Begin with gratitude**: Gratitude goes a long way in lifting your spirit, boosting your mood, reducing stress, and improving your relationships. Take a moment to give thanks by writing down a few things you're grateful for, meditating, or saying a prayer.

4. **Get moving**: There are amazing benefits to moving your body in the mornings. Some are improved focus, less stress, and more energy. If you feel energized in the mornings and you have the time, then schedule a morning workout. If not, do a quick stretch or walk outside. Don't forget to stay hydrated!

5. **Bring out your to-do list**: This should have been written the night before but

fine-tuned in the morning. Get on with your tasks, starting from the most important to the least. Doing this will help you feel more in control of your day.

6. **Wake up fifteen minutes earlier**: If time still feels too short and everything rushed, you can set your alarm to wake up fifteen minutes earlier than usual. That extra fifteen minutes can give you a better headstart on your day and make you feel more in control. Be sure to spend that time doing something for you.

30-Day Challenge

Day One: Whip out your notepad tonight and create your to-do list for tomorrow. Once done, look for what you can do right now that will make tomorrow morning less hectic, like cleaning the kitchen, laying out your clothes/the children's clothes, and packing your gym bag. Do them immediately and strike them off your list. Be sure to keep your journal/notepad by your bedside.

Day Two: Before getting out of bed, say a "Thank you" prayer the moment you open your eyes. If you prefer to write, get your journal and write down five things for which you are grateful. Start with the privilege of being alive and list four other reasons.

Chapter 2:

Tool Number 2: Relieve Stress and Negative Energy

Stress is one word we women are all too familiar with. It's the physical, mental, or emotional drain that could leave a person feeling angry or irritated.

A little science for you: When we feel stressed, our hypothalamus-pituitary-adrenal (HPA) axis is triggered, and some hormones (including the stress hormone cortisol) are released to help us respond to our stressors. This puts our bodies into the fight-or-flight mode.

Stress is not always bad. A good amount of stress in your body can help you improve your performance. Prolonged stress, however, can lead to several diseases like heart disease and mental health problems, including anxiety and depression. So, it is important to learn effective ways to help you relieve stress from the hustle and bustle of life's journey.

To manage stress, you must first identify the root causes: *What is draining you mentally or emotionally? Is it your relationship with someone? Is it your workload? Are there situations that usually trigger your stress response?*

Once you can identify what is causing you to feel stressed out, classify it. *Can it be solved? Is it something that will get better over time? Or is it irreversible and not worth the stress at all?*

Next, adjust your lifestyle to handle it better. Seek ways to become productive. Prioritize chores. Delegate duties. Strike a balance. (more on these in Tool Number 11).

Do you know how some people seem to drain

the life out of you? You may not be able to place it, but you can feel it whenever you're around them — they just have negative energy! Sometimes, their negative energy sticks with you, and before you know it, you're being negative too. It is your duty to protect your spirit and mental health by ridding yourself of any negative energy they may have transferred to you. Here are five pathways to cleanse negative energy from your spirit and body:

1. **Meditate daily:** Meditation is a great stress reliever. When you meditate, you are examining your thought patterns without passing any form of judgment. It is therapeutic and can be used to bring your body and mind back into harmony.

2. **Explore nature:** Nature therapy is an effective way to cleanse your body and mind. Immerse yourself in the beautiful

scenery by the mountains, woods, or oceans.

3. **Get moving:** When you move, like exercising, you release energy from your body. Negative energy thrives when you are inactive.

4. **Quit complaining:** If you have a habit of complaining, you must realize it is toxic. It keeps you stuck in a negative feedback loop. Quit complaining and choose gratitude instead.

5. **Smile often:** Smiling helps your body release negative energy. When you smile, neuropeptides are produced. They help to reduce stress, lower blood pressure, and improve your mood.

30-Day Challenge

Day Three: It's meditation time! Think of

something you want to meditate on, like a thought, quote, phrase, or anything at all. Find a quiet spot and sit with your eyes closed. Take a deep breath for four seconds, saying "breathe in" in your mind as you do it. Exhale deeply for another four seconds and say, "Breathe out" in your mind. Focus on your preferred thought and keep it there. When your mind begins to wander (because it surely will), bring yourself back to focus. Sit there for at least five minutes. When done, be still and quiet to hear what the universe might say to you.

Day Four: Today, go to a local park, mountainside, river, or anywhere with beautiful scenery. Pay attention to nature's gift to us as you explore the trees, flowers, waters, etc. Take pictures of anything that amuses you, and feel free to journal your thoughts as they come up.

Day Five: Set a reminder on your phone with the caption, "Smile!!!" You can make it an hourly reminder that whenever it beeps, you know what to do immediately — smile!

Chapter 3:

Tool Number 3: Affirm Yourself Daily

To eliminate negativity, you'll need some positivity! One great way to be positive is to affirm yourself.

In my 365 affirmations book, *The Fearless Journey,* I define positive affirmations as simple and short phrases that, when repeated daily, can change how you think and feel about yourself. This statement is so true. Positive affirmations can help you combat negativity and push you towards achieving your goals and manifesting your dreams and visions if you say them daily. Just try it!

The human mind is such a wonder, and what

you feed it continuously is what will stick. If you were raised in a dysfunctional family system, which has negatively shaped your perception of yourself and life, there is still hope for you. You can break out of negative cycles by learning to reprogram your subconscious mind.

For affirmations to work for you, you'll need to master the art of hearing your thoughts and repositioning them if they don't align with your desired outcome. So, start by asking yourself these questions: *What do I believe? Why do I believe what I believe?*

Your answers to the above questions will help you become more self-aware of your subconscious thought patterns. Then, you can begin the process of breaking free from negative thoughts by replacing them with positive ones. These are a few ways you can practice saying positive affirmations:

- Consider an area of your life where you desire growth/change, such as your self-esteem, and write out the negative self-talk you've gotten used to. Perhaps you struggle with insecurities about your appearance and personality and have always called yourself "stupid" or "less-than." Write that down.

- After writing out the negative self-talk, rewrite it by changing it to something positive. In this case, your goal is to change your perception of yourself from less-than to worthy. Use present tense and construct the language to reflect what you want rather than what you don't want. For instance, say, "I am made for this," instead of "I'm not too bad at this," and "I carry myself gracefully" instead of "I am not clumsy and scattered."

- Repeat the affirmations daily — morning and night. Say them out loud and look at yourself in a mirror.

- After committing to repeating it daily for about a month, evaluate yourself: *Do you feel better about yourself? Has your confidence improved? What is your mood like now that you have ditched negative self-talk?*

- Once you've done the evaluation, see how best you can refine your affirmations. Measure your progress and adjust your affirmations accordingly. Experiment with variations that speak to your goals, and remain consistent.

30-Day Challenge

Day Six: Let's do a bit of introspection today. Spend time evaluating your thought patterns

and answer the following questions in your
journal:

1. *What do I believe about myself?*
2. *What events in my childhood influenced this belief about myself?*
3. *Do these beliefs about myself reflect the real truth or a lie? Explain how.*
4. *What am I most worried about?*
5. *What mindset has hindered me from doing all I truly desire to do?*
6. *How can a positive mindset help with my transformation?*

Day Seven: Create your own affirmations by writing down the negative things you may have believed about yourself and then rewriting them to the positive version. Be very specific. For instance, if you have negative self-talk like, "I'm never gonna succeed anyways…" change it to, "Success is my birthright. I am successful in this business!" Once written, stand in front of the mirror and repeat it to yourself every morning and night.

Day Eight: Get creative by recording your voice saying the affirmations. Have it on your phone so that anytime negative self-talk creeps into your mind, you can plug your ears and listen to yourself speaking. Repeat the affirmations as you listen.

Chapter 4:
Tool Number 4: Nourish Your Body

One way to nourish your body is by giving it the proper meals for growth and overall health.

Proper meals refer to eating foods that are loaded with wholesome macronutrients (carbs, proteins, and fats) and micronutrients (minerals and vitamins).

Nourishing your body is non-negotiable when going on a transformation journey because you need good food to function—no one does well when *hungry!*

Let me be clear that nourishing your body

doesn't mean dieting. The diet culture has made a mess of our eating habits — telling us to restrict one food group or the other and calling foods "good" and "bad." This is not what I am talking about. Nourishing your body with food is more about prioritizing the foods that are packed with nutrients while occasionally enjoying those that may not have as many benefits. The secret is balance.

Nourishing your body with good food has amazing benefits. Some of these benefits include:

- It provides energy for activities and powers fundamental processes like breathing and digestion.
- It boosts your immune system and helps to heal your bones, muscles, and other tissues.
- It reduces your chances of chronic

illnesses and preserves your overall health and well-being.

- It helps you get to your preferred healthy weight and maintain it.
- It keeps your skin glowing, allowing you to age with grace.

Here are two major food-related ways to nourish your body for your transformation:

#1. Practice Mindful Eating: Mindful eating means being fully present when you're eating. It involves paying close attention to your body — noticing how the food makes you feel, savoring the taste, and watching out for signals indicating fullness and satisfaction — whenever you eat. Mindful eating is a non-judgmental approach to eating, and it is beneficial because it gives you a greater appreciation for life and the ability to eat what you want. It also makes digestion easier, improving your general health and well-being.

You can practice mindful eating by removing distractions (like the T.V. or your phone) during meal times, focusing on the food and chewing slowly, and taking note of the taste of all the components of the food.

#2. Eat A Variety of Foods: There are five food groups: grains, proteins, fruits and vegetables, dairy, and fats;

- Grains: Grains give you fiber, and fiber is great because it keeps you fuller for longer, helps to ease bowel movement, and lowers high blood pressure. Some sources of grains are brown rice, oats, quinoa, and popcorn.

- Proteins: Proteins are great for building and repairing your muscles. Some protein foods include poultry, fish, lean meats, nuts, and soy-based products.

- Fruits and Vegetables: These contain vital minerals, vitamins, and plant chemicals that help protect you against diseases like cancer and diabetes.

- Dairy: Dairy is great for bone strength, and fermented foods (like cheese and yogurt) have healthy gut bacteria that could benefit your digestive health.

- Fats: Fats give your body energy, help you absorb some vital nutrients, and so much more. Opt for more unsaturated sources of fat like avocado, nuts and seeds, and olive oil.

Please note that your body will also benefit from other types of nourishment, like adequate sleep and exercise. Tools 8 and 10 will discuss these two concepts, respectively.

30-Day Challenge

Day Nine: Make your grocery shopping list. Be sure to include mostly foods that are packed with nutrients and less processed ones. Make a firm determination to stick with your list when you go grocery shopping.

Day Ten: Choose a convenient time and meal of the day to practice mindful eating. Serve yourself the portion you think will satisfy you. Sit at the dining table without any distractions. Take a spoon/fork of the meal and chew for about twenty seconds. As you chew, think about how each component of the meal tastes. Give thanks for the food.

Chapter 5:
Tool Number 5: Self-Love = Self-Care

Self-love is a deep appreciation of yourself. This appreciation can mean different things to each person because we all have unique ways of showing it. However, one thing must remain the same with self-love: a person who loves themselves will show it by prioritizing and doing the things that promote their overall well-being — in other words, they will practice self-care.

It is critical to love yourself for your overall well-being. In fact, you cannot transform into this amazing, successful woman without first loving yourself. Self-love will be the driving force on your journey to becoming the best version of yourself.

So, if I may ask: *Do you really love yourself?* I'm talking about the kind of love that is evident in what you say to yourself and what you do to yourself.

Self-care simply means caring for your physical, mental, and emotional well-being. It involves taking a holistic approach to nurturing yourself because you love yourself enough to do what is best for you.

There are four pillars of self-care: spiritual, mental, emotional, and physical.

#1. Spiritual Self-care is your personal journey to connecting with your highest self. Spirituality can mean different things to everyone, from religion to culture to nature. Spiritual self-care seeks to find purpose in doing things for the greater good, like being generous, meditating, attending religious services, or exploring nature.

#2. Mental Self-Care involves caring for your mental health (thought patterns and mindset). Here, you're paying attention to what feeds your mind and stimulates your brain. You can practice mental self-care by journaling, practicing gratitude, reading wholesome content, and doing puzzles.

#3. Emotional Self-Care is more about catering to one's emotional needs. It involves accepting one's feelings without judgment, developing emotional awareness, and creating boundaries.

#4. Physical Self-Care is attending to your body's physical needs, such as staying hydrated, going for regular medical check-ups, making healthy food choices, and staying physically active.

You can cultivate self-love by doing the following:

- **Embrace your uniqueness:** It can feel tempting to want to conform to society's standards of what you should look like and who you should be. But don't fall for it. You are unique and deserve to find expression through your uniqueness. You have no reason to wallow in comparison and apologize for being you.

- **Develop self-awareness:** Self-awareness helps you to evaluate your emotions objectively—why you feel the way you do, what you're feeling, and how to manage it. It is one of the most vital emotional skills a woman can have. When you develop your self-awareness, you'll know the value of self-love—you'll learn your love language and show compassion toward yourself.

- **Engage in self-care routines:** Make time to cater to the four pillars of self-care. Focus on building your spirit, nurturing your soul (mind and emotions), and fueling your body appropriately. You can never go wrong when you prioritize self-care.

The truth is, no one just wakes up and decides not to love themselves. Most times, we genuinely want to love ourselves but don't know how, or we find ourselves constantly struggling with behaviors that hinder us from putting this love into action. It is time to be real with your- self and know that you cannot succeed without self-love and self-care.

30-Day Challenge

Day Eleven: Let's focus on spiritual self-care today. Search for a podcast that focuses on spiritual content. Listen to at least one episode. It could be content related to your religion or belief systems. After doing that, meditate on whatever you learn from it.

Day Twelve: Today is for mental self-care. Give your mind a break from all the noise. Read a book about something new and jot down everything you learn.

Day Thirteen: It's time for emotional self-care. Speak with a close friend, mentor, counselor, therapist, or health and lifestyle coach. Talk to them about things you might be struggling with.

Day Fourteen: Now to physical self-care. Attend a fitness class today. If you cannot go out to a gym, check for a video online and follow along. While at it, be sure to drink some water. After the class, take a cool/warm bath to relax your body.

Chapter 6:
Tool Number 6: Forgive

We cannot go through life without experiencing hurt of various degrees and magnitudes. Humans are a work in progress, meaning that we will never do everything perfectly, and offenses will surely come. Sometimes, you will be the offender, too. But no matter what hurt we have faced (and will still face in the future), we must forgive to free ourselves from bitterness and hatred.

Forgiveness can be a very sensitive topic, especially for women who may have faced hurts that caused deep soul wounds. However, one thing we must note about forgiveness is that it benefits you more than the other person. So, forgiveness should never be an option. It must be a priority.

To forgive means to intentionally set aside any negative emotions or resentment toward someone who has wronged you. Forgiveness does not mean that what the offender did is okay or acceptable but that you choose to let it go because you want to live an unhindered life—spiritually, emotionally, mentally, and even physically.

Letting go could be very difficult, and quite frankly, some wounds take a long time for us to heal and recover from. We may not even forget them entirely, but at least they will have less of an effect on us than before we began our healing journey. Think of it as a scar from a big accident. Over the years, the pain will subside, but the scar might remain forever.

Counselors and therapists acknowledge forgiveness as a crucial first step in recovery and personal transformation. Research shows that those who forgive experience significantly less stress and mental health conditions. Even spiritual guides will tell you that forgiveness is your pathway to healing. Need I say more?

You might wonder: *If someone hurt me this badly, why should I forgive them?*

As I said before, forgiveness benefits you more than the offender. When you hold on to hurt/resentment/bitterness/hatred, it prevents your soul from finding peace. Living a life without true peace is chaotic. And this chaos in your soul can manifest in the body, too.

Unforgiveness puts your body under stress — your heart starts racing faster when you think about or see the offender, your mind is clogged with negativity, and you're unable to function freely at your best. On the flip side, forgiveness puts your body and mind at ease, giving you an improved well-being.

Please note that reconciliation and forgiveness are two separate concepts. You can forgive and let go without reconciling with an offender, especially someone likely to hurt you again. For instance, a woman can forgive her partner, who was constantly physically abusive to her. However, she may not seek reconciliation if that puts her at risk of being physically abused by them again.

In all honesty, forgiveness might not fix all relationships right away, but at least it remains an essential first step for you to heal and keep thriving. If you've been struggling with forgiving and letting go of hurt, here are steps you can take to forgive:

1. **Talk to someone:** When we hold things in our hearts and minds, they have the tendency to weigh us down. It is helpful to talk to someone, like a therapist, counselor, close friend, or mentor, about deep soul wounds. Just letting it out can offer some relief.

2. **Evaluate your lessons:** While painful events can make you see only the bad, they usually have hidden lessons ingrained. Ponder on the experience and highlight the lessons learned. *Has it made you wiser? Have you now learned more about yourself? Can you see areas where you need improvement?* There will always be something to take away, even from hurtful experiences.

3. **Start small:** Begin by forgiving minor issues. When "little" offenses arise, practice releasing them in your mind.

That way, it may not be daunting to let go of more significant hurt.

4. **Say, "I forgive you.":** Words have power. When someone offends you, the offense can keep replaying in your mind, weighing you down and causing you to feel angrier. When that happens, open your mouth and say out loud, "I forgive you!" You can also write an "I forgive you" letter to the offender. This letter is for your eyes only, except if you really feel that you must share it with them. Writing it down helps you to release all the negative energy from your body and soul.

5. **Practice compassion:** Always remember this: People who hurt people are usually hurt and wounded themselves. Wounds have a way of scaring us so badly that we become numb to other

people's pains. Therefore, we may do things without realizing the impact on the other person. Those who do hurtful things are usually just operating from their woundedness. So, try to look at situations with a new lens. *Maybe they didn't mean it… maybe they had no idea how much it would affect me… maybe they're not in the right frame of mind.* Just maybe. When you practice compassion, it can help you let go of the offense.

Sometimes, the person you need to forgive is yourself. You might be carrying guilt, shame, and condemnation towards yourself for what you did or did not do. This is equally very unhealthy. It is time to take the steps above to forgive yourself so that you can live life to the fullest.

30-Day Challenge

Day Fifteen: Write your own "I forgive you" letter to the person who hurt you. Don't filter anything. Let all your emotions out, and do not judge yourself as you do.

Day Sixteen: Your letter yesterday was the first step to letting go. Today, try visualizing forgiveness. Sit on a chair with your eyes closed and visualize the offender sitting in front of you. Next, get up and drop the pain (imagine the pain is a heavy load you're carrying) onto the floor. Leave it there and look the person in the eyes and say:

I choose to forgive you right now. I am letting go of the hurt and pain you caused me. I will not hold you in contempt in my thoughts, words, or actions. I forgive you, and now, I am free to live my life to the fullest.

Stay quiet for 20 seconds as your body and

soul release the negative emotions. Then, walk

away.

Chapter 7:
Tool Number 7: Own Your Goals

What are your life goals? Do you have them written out? Are you on track with each milestone? Are you doing anything to measure your progress?

I can guess that becoming successful is one of your goals—or why else would you be reading this book? Well, that's great! However, many times, goals simply remain wishful thinking because people don't get up and do the work. So, the big question is: Are you ready to do the work?

Goal setting is visualizing what your future

should be like and inspiring yourself to make that future happen. It is a specific and effective tool to help take you from where you are right now to where you want to be. If you don't set goals, you can remain stagnant in your personal and professional development, you will burn out quickly due to taking on too much or feeling overwhelmed by unstructured tasks, and you will have no way to measure your progress. So, setting your goals on your path to success is very important.

Here's how to start setting your personal goals:

Firstly, you want to evaluate your long-term goals. *Where do you want to be in a decade?* Write out everything you can picture in the future. For example, in ten years, I see myself running a global coaching business for women who desire personal development.

Next, break down these long-term goals into short-term goals. *What can you do now that will add up to what you want to see in the future?* To become a successful women's coach, I need to become certified. What certification courses can I take? How can I gain experience right now? How can I find women that I can coach for free for a start? The answers to these questions will help you draw up your short-term goals.

It is impossible to talk about goals without mentioning the SMART goals framework by George T. Doran. Your goals need to be:

- **S**pecific: For my goal to be effective, it must be specific. What do I specifically want to accomplish? Who is responsible for it? What specific steps can I take?

- **M**easurable: How can I quantify or measure my goals to ensure that I am on track to reach the finish line? What milestones can I create within different timeframes?

- **A**chievable: Here is the reality check-point - is my objective something I can reasonably accomplish within this timeframe?

- **R**elevant: Now, the bigger picture - why am I setting this goal? For what purpose?

- **T**ime-bound: To measure success, you must set timeframes for completing the milestones. By doing this, you'll be able to stay on track and overcome procrastination.

When you write out your goals, see that they fit into the SMART framework.

Speaking of writing, let us briefly look at journaling—a highly effective way to keep up with your thoughts!

When you journal, you document your ideas and emotions, allowing you to better process and understand them. Journaling is a necessary habit to develop, as it helps you become more self-aware.

The beauty of journaling is its flexibility. You can choose from a variety of journaling styles, such as daily journaling, visual journaling, gratitude journaling, or stream-of-consciousness journaling.

Here are a few steps to make journaling a habit:

1. **Get a journal:** Journals can be in a hard-copy notebook or an app on your phone. Just ensure you have something handy so you can remain consistent no matter where you are.

2. **Free yourself:** Avoid making edits; just write from your heart as it comes. It's for your eyes only. There is no right or wrong approach to this—no one is judging your grammar and spelling.

3. **Set a convenient time and space:** Create a schedule with a convenient time and space that you can maintain in the long run. Many women have journaled at some point, but it gets challenging to do it frequently. Therefore, it is vital to set a time of day for it. It could be first thing in the morning, during your lunch break, or last thing at night. Create a routine, set a reminder, and get it done.

4. **Use the internet:** When you feel stuck, search for journal prompts online to help you continue.

30-Day Challenge

Day Seventeen: Write your goals and fit them into the SMART Framework. Use the following questions below as a guide:

1. *What specific goal do you want to achieve within the next five years?*

2. *What can you do weekly/monthly/quarterly that adds up to meeting the big goal?*

3. *What action plan(s) do you have in place?*

4. *What can you achieve with the current resources available to you?*

5. *When will each milestone be due for completion?*

Day Eighteen: Do something specifically geared toward your big goal. It could be signing up for an online course in an area you want to improve on, going to the grocery store to get healthy foodstuff to begin your weight loss journey, or meeting up with a business mentor to discuss your business ideas.

Day Nineteen: Search for journal prompts online or buy a guided journal book that you can use to assist with journaling your thoughts daily.

Chapter 8:
Tool Number 8: Rest

If we paid more attention to rest, we would be in a better mental and physical state. Rest is a non-negotiable aspect of success. Our bodies were not created to keep working overdrive. They need a buffer period to recuperate and regain optimal functioning.

When you prioritize rest, even if for a brief moment, it helps renew you throughout your day. This renewal improves your overall well-being. Rest allows your body to repair and maintain balance, especially after a lack of sleep (more on sleep in the next section) or exposure to high-stress levels.

It might surprise you to know that rest improves creativity. Do you want your creativity to flow abundantly? Get some rest! Rest replenishes your mental reserves and encourages reflection. It enhances brain connectivity, allowing your creative ideas to flow.

Rest helps your mental productivity. Your brain, like your muscles, will function better once it has adequate rest. You may have realized that you always struggle with tasks at certain times of the day. This could be a clear indication that you are worn out and need a moment to rest and refresh before getting back to the task.

Rest improves decision-making by providing a fresh viewpoint. You might have heard people say something like, "Let me sleep on it." This is so true because rest helps to renew your mind, increasing attention and emotional capacity.

Some ways to include rest in your daily life
are:

- Set a goal to take five deep breaths at
  different intervals of your day.
- Try relaxing exercises like yoga or
  stretching. Prioritize sleep.

Sleep is another form of nourishment that you
need. It is vital for your mind and body to re-
charge, keeping you feeling refreshed and
alert upon waking. Not getting enough sleep
disturbs brain function and affects concentra-
tion, clarity of thought, and memory pro-
cessing.

As adults, we need a recommended seven to
nine hours of sleep each night. I know this can
be a tall order for some women, especially
moms of young children. You cannot always
control the different factors that might cut

your sleep hours, but you can adopt some tips to encourage better sleep:

- Ditch your phone/screens at least thirty minutes before bedtime.

- Create a "wind down" routine that involves taking a shower, dimming the lights, playing soft music, doing a quick stretch, and meditation.

- Be cautious of what you eat and when you eat. Avoid taking heavy meals, alcohol, or caffeine close to bedtime. Even though alcohol might make you feel sleepy initially, it tends to disrupt sleep later.

- Include exercise in your daily routine, but not too close to bedtime.

- Manage your thoughts. Resolve issues earlier in the day or at least before you sleep. Clear your mind of anxieties and worries by journaling, praying, or meditating on wholesome content. A crowded mind can hamper your ability to sleep soundly.

30-Day Challenge

Day Twenty: Create your "wind down" routine. Think of things you can do just before you sleep, like deep breathing/meditation/prayer, stretching, journaling, playing music, etc. Ensure that items in your routine are things you will enjoy doing. It will be challenging to keep up with it if they're not.

Day Twenty-One: Resolve any issues you have with someone. Call them up, meet with them, or send them a message apologizing if you wronged them.

Day Twenty-Two: Start following your "wind-down" routine (paying close attention to all the above tips) and see what difference it makes after two weeks.

Chapter 9:

Tool Number 9: Mindset and Motivation

You are what you believe, and your beliefs are formed by your most dominant thoughts. So, what is your most dominant thought about yourself? Do you know that *that* thought makes up your mindset— affecting how you view and respond to people and life's circumstances?

Your mindset is a set of beliefs that influence your vision of the world and yourself. It influences your thoughts, emotions, and behavior, and it plays a significant role in your success or failure.

Renowned American Psychologist Carol

Dweck discovered that humans have two main mindsets regarding success: a growth mindset and a fixed mindset.

In a fixed mindset, a person sees their abilities as unchangeable. Such a person will rely only on natural talent for success, ignoring the importance of effort. They don't bother taking on new things or stretching themselves outside their "usual." They live by *'it's either I'm good at this, or I'm not.'*

In contrast, a person with a growth mindset recognizes the opportunity for success through focus and determination. They may not expect to become a genius in everything, but they see potential for skill and intelligent development through constant work. Such a person will spend time mastering their talent and learning new skills. They take setbacks as stepping stones to do even better next time and are intentional about their growth process.

Their motto is *I can learn to do anything I set my mind to.*

Which mindset would you rather have?

If you really want to succeed, you need to have a growth mindset. It doesn't pay to limit yourself in any way. Those who have made a significant impact in life have pushed beyond their limits! So, it is time for you to develop a growth mindset and make success happen for yourself, and here are a few tips to do just that:

1. **Implement self-care activities you can do daily:** Focus on building your spirit, nurturing your soul (mind and emotions), and fueling your body appropriately. These will help to feed you the right mindset.

2. **Step outside of your comfort zone:** Have you been limiting yourself lately? It's about time to remove those

limitations and try something different. Expand your worldview in areas of your life that you have remained re-stricted. Face your fears and overcome them.

3. **Accept setbacks when they come and adapt to change:** Failure is not the end unless you let it be. When things go wrong, sit back and analyze all the les-sons you learned from the process. Em-brace those lessons and look forward to another opportunity to improve.

4. **Be on the lookout for inspiration and motivation every day:** Seek motivation and inspiration from various healthy sources, such as music, documentaries, or reading inspiring materials. These sources can help you overcome self-doubts and keep you motivated.

Motivation gets you started on your

transformation journey and keeps you moving toward your goals. It is that invisible power that drives and sustains your endeavors.

You can find motivation from two major sources: extrinsic and intrinsic.

Extrinsic motivation happens when rewards such as prizes, praise, or money come from outside of you. They are external incentives that motivate you to keep doing what you are doing. For instance, you might remain motivated to complete a project mainly because of the money you'll get once it is done. Extrinsic motivation is not bad. However, it should not be the only source you rely on because when those things are not available, you might give up on your goals.

Intrinsic motivation—the opposite of extrinsic—is motivation that comes from within you. It is when you do things mainly because of the internal pleasure and fulfillment you derive from them rather than because of a reward you want to get from someone else. This is a great type of motivation that women need to succeed.

30-Day Challenge

Day Twenty-Three: Call a friend, colleague, or the closest person to you and ask them to give you honest feedback on how you speak. Ask them if you often sound negative or positive. Ask them if they feel you give your best to achieve your goals. Sometimes, you may not know your weaknesses until someone else points it out. Take note of their feedback and actively seek ways to improve.

Day Twenty-Four: Let's push the limits today. What is that one thing you've always imagined doing but haven't had the courage to go after it? Drop the fears and excuses, and go for it today!

Chapter 10:
Tool Number 10: Exercise and Endorphins

Previously, we looked at nutrition and sleep as nourishment for our bodies. There is one other nourishment that we need—exercise. Exercise is great for you because of the many benefits to your mental and physical health.

We all have some hormones known as the "feel-good or happy hormones," like dopamine, serotonin, and endorphins. Dopamine is associated with pleasurable feelings, learning, memory, and so on. Serotonin helps regulate your mood, sleep, appetite, and so on. And endorphins serve as your body's natural pain reliever, produced in response to discomfort or stress.

Exercising regularly can boost your body's production of these hormones — dopamine, serotonin, and endorphins. When that happens, your mood is regulated, you'll feel less stressed, have better sleep at night, and much more.

Working out regularly can help strengthen your muscles and bones. The older you get, the more muscle you lose and the weaker your bones become, increasing your chances of injury. When exercise is a part of your daily life, you prevent your muscles and bones from deteriorating quickly.

Exercise also boosts your energy levels. Let's face it: if you want to go after any success goals, you'll need mental and physical energy. Exercise can play a crucial role in improving cardiovascular health—pumping more blood to your heart and supplying your muscles with energy, making you stronger and more energized to go after your tasks.

Additionally, if you need to lose weight, adding a workout program to your weight loss plan will help you achieve great results. In all, exercise is a great way to improve your overall health and well-being. And look, you only have one body to live in, so why not take good care of it? Here's how to make exercise more enjoyable and sustainable for you:

1. **Ditch comparison:** Building or maintaining an exercise routine will be unique to you. We all have different fitness levels, and our bodies respond differently to exercise. So, avoid comparing yourself with your neighbor or that fitness influencer who works out three

hours a day or lost 60 pounds in three months. Do what you can and appreciate your progress.

2. **Start small:** You don't need the biggest equipment to start exercising. Start with that small space beside your bed and your body weight, and keep at it. You also don't need to wait until you have an hour at your disposal. Work out in fifteen minutes, and you'll feel energized.

3. **Set goals:** Set goals to improve your fitness. If you can afford it, sign up at a gym and get a personal trainer to work closely with you to achieve your goals.

4. **Choose activities wisely:** It is difficult to remain consistent at something you don't enjoy. Your body can get a good workout in several ways, so choose activities that relate to your interest and

skill level. If you love dancing, join a dance fitness class or follow a dance fitness video/program on social media. If you enjoy horseback riding, then take that up. There is no one way to get fit!

5. **Plan the timing:** Some women enjoy working out really early while others don't. Figure out what timing works best for you, and schedule that period to do your workouts. The more convenient the time, the better your chances of sticking with the routine.

6. **Always warm up and cool down:** Exercising without warming up or cooling down can cause injuries. When injuries become frequent, you may be discouraged from continuing to exercise.

7. **Monitor how your body feels:** If you feel a lot of discomfort or pain at some point, that might signify that you're

doing too much. Adjust your routine and watch how your body responds. Pushing through too much discomfort or pain can lead to serious injuries, which can prevent you from consistently working out.

8. **Reward yourself:** Always find ways to reward yourself for being consistent. Reward, in this sense, does not have to be food-related. You can soak in a warm bubble bath, go to the spa, or watch your favorite show. Rewarding yourself gives you more motivation to keep going.

9. **Get an accountability partner.** Your accountability partner could be your personal trainer, workout buddy, friend, or mentor. Share your goals with that person and let them monitor your progress.

30-Day Challenge

Day Twenty-Five: Create your fitness goals for the next twelve months. Outline what you want to achieve monthly, and set reasonable action plans. For example, you might want to lose twenty pounds in twelve months. Set a goal to exercise for 30 minutes five times a week (prioritizing strength training exercises). Don't forget to optimize your nutrition to get adequate protein for muscle building!

Day Twenty-Six: Get an accountability partner and give them a copy of your goals. Report daily to them, letting them know what you ate and how much exercise you got. Give them permission to push you to achieve these goals.

Day Twenty-Seven: Find creative ways to incorporate more movement into your day. Opt for the stairs rather than the convenience of the elevator. Take a stroll to the grocery store instead of hopping behind the wheel. Do twenty jumping jacks during commercials. Just be creative!

Chapter 11:

Tool Number 11: Discipline, Distractions, and Doing Hard Things First

W e may all dread the "d" word, but truth be told, success will not happen until discipline is in place. Discipline is the ability to control your behavior by obeying certain rules and standards. It means following a set of rules based on your values and beliefs. It's an intentional way of living.

A disciplined woman will have many desirable character traits, such as determination, independence, motivation, organization, focus, resilience, responsibility, confidence, and steadfastness. Think about any highly successful, influential, and inspiring woman in history. These are all qualities you will find in her.

Self-discipline might sound like boring stuff because it can make you feel limited or confined. But it is time to see it as a priceless trait that sets you apart from the average woman who does not strive for success. Self-discipline is non-negotiable if you want to hop on and remain on the forward-progressing train. With self-discipline, you'll be able to overlook distractions and do the hard things first.

Here are a few reasons why self-discipline is a badass trait to develop right now:

1. **Achievement of goals:** Setting goals is one thing. Achieving those goals is another. Self-discipline will help you keep up with your goals, giving you the

focus and determination to push past setbacks.

2. **Decision-making:** It's easy to be swayed by your emotions even when you know you shouldn't. Self-discipline helps you assess situations before making decisions (especially crucial ones), allowing you to make the right decision at the right time and avoid impulsive choices that may not benefit your well-being.

3. **Improves efficiency:** If you want to be productive—getting on with things that must be done—you need self-discipline. It can help you manage time and plan more effectively.

4. **Resilience and perseverance:** Life's hard. Unplanned circumstances will pop up every now and then. You'll need to know how to bounce back from

setbacks. Self-discipline will help you achieve this.

5. **Strengthens relationships:** No one enjoys being friends with a woman whose emotions are always *all over the place.* Self-discipline helps you better manage your emotions in response to other people's words and actions, strengthening relationships.

6. **Improves mental and physical health:** Do you want to make healthy choices like eating right and exercising regularly? Do you want to sharpen your mind? You'll need self-discipline to achieve these!

7. **Lives on purpose:** A self-disciplined woman will have a deep sense of purpose. She will live with the consciousness that life is short and an impact needs to be made now.

I bet by now you want to know how to develop this trait. So, here are some tips for becoming self-disciplined:

- Establish clear goals—write them down, and have them where you can see them.
- Draw up a plan outlining the steps required to achieve your goals.
- Practice how to prioritize what's important. Practice self-control by removing distractions. Establish a steady daily routine.
- Get an accountability partner like a friend or coach.

Sometimes, you might find yourself pushing the hard tasks away. This can become a habit called procrastination. Procrastination is a major enemy of success. It's important to face your tasks head-on to reach your goal. Here are a few tips to help you quit procrastinating:

- First, acknowledge that you have an issue with either not doing important tasks or leaving them incomplete.

- Evaluate why this happens. *Do you find that most of your time is devoted to less important things? Is the task tedious or overwhelming? Do you fear failing or succeeding?* Be sure to establish your "why."

- Rewire your mind by choosing positive self-talk over negative ones. Simply saying, "I can get it done right now," instead of "I can't do this. It's all too much for me!"

- Break down big tasks into smaller portions. Then, choose one that you can address immediately.

- Be very specific with your schedule. Assign times or dates to important tasks and start with the most pressing.

- Adjust your environment to allow you to focus. Take distractions like screens away for specific durations.

- Be kind to yourself. You're not going to get a hang of it immediately. So, when you drop the ball, pick it up again and keep moving.

30-Day Challenge

Day Twenty-Eight: Evaluate all the tasks you have outlined. Which ones have you been avoiding/procrastinating on? Face the undone or uncompleted tasks and begin working on them immediately. Don't stop until you're done or you know that you physically and mentally cannot continue.

Day Twenty-Nine: Let's try a self-discipline game. Buy something you really like to have or use and keep it where your eyes can see it. Make up your mind not to have/use it for the next five to fifteen days. You can make the game more challenging by deciding not to even touch or look in the direction of the item. See how long it takes you before you lose your self-discipline!

Day Thirty: End this challenge with gratitude. Take stock of all that you've done these past thirty days and appreciate yourself for your tenacity. Listen to a "thank you" song.

Afterword

Congratulations on completing your **30-day "TRANSFORMED" Challenge**! You have just taken a huge step towards transforming into the woman of your dreams, and I'm super proud of you!

Quick question: How do you feel? Seriously, write down your thoughts in your journal.

You know what? I wish I were in front of you right now, looking you in the eye and saying proudly, "Well done!" for your effort. You slayed!

Over the past month, you've learned new ways to improve your overall health and well-being and increase your chances of huge success by using my **TRANSFORMED**

Framework. You have pushed beyond your previously perceived limits and finally seen that diligent work pays. You must be over the moon right now, and quite deservedly so!

Now that the challenge is done, I need you to understand that this is not the end. In fact, it's only the beginning.

So, first, spend some time reflecting on the entire experience:

What have you learned about yourself and your abilities? What were the most notable changes you made? What were the toughest tools, and how did you manage to overcome them?

When you take ample time to reflect, you'll be better equipped to maintain your progress and continue improving.

Now that you have built a solid foundation, I need you to keep chasing those dreams with everything in you. Use all you've learned to create a sustainable plan for your future. Set your SMART goals with actionable plans to achieve them. You have all the tools you need at your fingertips (and in this book). Use them!

It's important to note that nobody is perfect. Your success journey will not be straightfor-ward. There will be days when you just cannot find the motivation to do something produc-tive or make healthy lifestyle choices, and that's totally okay. Remember to be compas-sionate toward yourself and avoid giving in to negative self-talk, like judgment or criticism. After such moments, reflect on what triggered those lethargic feelings and see how to avoid them next time.

Success comes with unique challenges. You may get to a level of success, thinking you've gotten it all under control, only to discover newer obstacles. Don't let these deter you.

Rather, see them as opportunities to build more resilience. Keep fighting back, and your capacity will keep increasing. You can take it!

Congratulations again on completing this challenge. You did it. Now, go out there and become the next successful woman the whole world will be talking about for generations to come. I'll always be rooting for you!

All my love, Lauren Brentley

About the Author

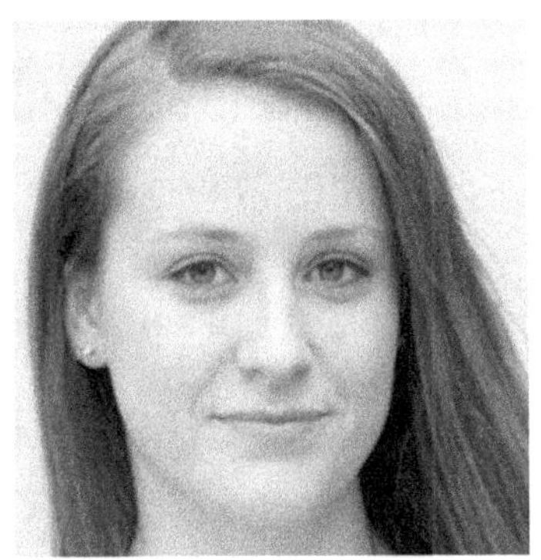

Lauren Brentley, a 35-year-old personal development enthusiast, is the author of "The Art of Doing Hard Things First: Strategies for Women to Overcome Procrastination, Create Positive Habits and Achieve Success Now." With a passion for self-improvement and helping others, Lauren has devoted her life to inspiring and empowering women to overcome obstacles and achieve their goals.

As a single mother to a teenage daughter, Lauren understands the unique challenges that women face in balancing their personal and professional lives. Her experiences as a working mother have fueled her desire to create tools and strategies to help others find success, happiness, and fulfillment.

Lauren is an avid reader of self-help books and a firm believer in the power of positive thinking. In her free time, she enjoys working out and staying active, which she believes is essential for maintaining a healthy body and mind. She is also a strong advocate for lifelong learning and personal growth.

In "The Art of Doing Hard Things First," Lauren shares her insights, strategies, and personal experiences to help women overcome procrastination, develop positive habits, and set themselves on the path to success. Drawing on her own journey as a working mother and personal development enthusiast, Lauren provides practical advice and actionable steps that can be easily incorporated into any woman's daily routine.

Her dedication to empowering women and her passion for personal development are evident in her writing. Her unique perspective, born out of her own experiences and challenges, makes her an inspiring and relatable guide for women seeking to create lasting change and achieve their goals.

www.ingramcontent.com/pod-product-compliance
Lightning Source LLC
Chambersburg PA
CBHW070914160726
48004CB00003B/1368